ANGUS CALDER has been best known a
The People's War: Britain 1939-45 h
print since it appeared in 1969. Other substantial historical books fol-
lowed, and two collections of essays about Scotland, past and present.
But he has also published verse all his life, won a Gregory Award in
1967, and was convener of the Committee which helped Tessa Ransford
realise her vision of a Scottish Poetry Library in 1984.

Since he took early retirement from the Open University in Scotland
in 1993, he has written poetry more prolifically, and published widely.

His three previous collections are *Waking in Waikato* (1997),
Colours of Grief (2002) and *Dipa's Bowl* (2004). Receipt of a Scottish
Arts Council Writers Bursary in 2002 gave him gave him breathing space
to organise his uncollected verse, and this further book is one result. With
Luath Press he has also published *The Souls of the Dead are taking the
best seats: 50 world poets on war* (co-edited with Beth Junor, 2004) and
Scotlands of the Mind (2002).

Sun Behind the Castle

Edinburgh Poems

ANGUS CALDER

Luath Press Limited

EDINBURGH

www.luath.co.uk

First Published 2004

The author's right to be identified as author of this book under the
Copyright, Designs and Patents Acts 1988 has been asserted.

The publisher acknowledges subsidy from

 Scottish **Arts** Council

towards the publication of this book.

The paper used in this book is recyclable. It is made from low
chlorine pulps produced in a low energy, low emission manner
from renewable forests.

Printed and bound by
DiGiSource GB, Livingston

Typeset in Sabon 10.5 by
S Fairgrieve, Edinburgh 0131 658 1763

for CN

Contents

CONTENTS

Acknowledgements

MOST OF THESE POEMS have appeared in print before. Thanks to the editors of *Cencrastus*, *Chapman*, *The Dark Horse*, *Edinburgh History Graduates Association Newsletter*, *Groundswell*, *The Herald*, *Markings*, *Northwords*, *Outposts*, *Poetry Ireland Review*, *Poetry Scotland* and *Wasafiri*. 'Scott Monument' appeared in *Present Poets*, edited by Jenni Calder (National Museums of Scotland, 1998). Parts of 'Sequence in Cold Spring' were in *Friends and Kangaroos: New Writing Scotland 17*, edited by Moira Burgess and Donny O'Rourke (Association of Scottish Literary Studies, 1999). 'Small Game in Edinburgh Central' was in *Edinburgh: An Intimate City*, edited by Bashabi Fraser and Elaine Greig (City of Edinburgh Council, 2000).

Ten poems here are reprinted from my collection *Waking In Waikato* (diehard, 1998). 'Haymarket Sunset' and 'Salutations' appear in *Colours of Grief* (Shoestring, 2002) and 'For Joy Hendry', 'Thinking About Derek Walcott' and 'Armistice Day' in *Dipa's Bowl* (Aark Arts, 2004). *Horace in Tollcross* was published in 2000 as a pamphlet by James Robertson's Kettilonia Press. Pleasantly, it sold out in that form.

Thanks to all editors implicated above and once again, very special thanks to my former neighbours in Grindle's Bookshop, Sally Evans and Ian William King, of diehard publishers and *Poetry Scotland* magazine.

Introduction

IN A METROPOLITAN, departure-lounge world, with its inch-deep, multinational 'culture', a richer way of seeing – rooted, specific culture-fights for its place. These poems could not have been written anywhere but Edinburgh. This, the most beautiful, wry, challenging and haunting city in the British isles, with its 'classic grey – most delicious of lourdness, an ecstasy of glum' is the true hero/heroine of the pages that follow. These poems have the confidence and lightness of words at home in their own streets. In his concluding notes, Angus Calder embarks on a detailed analysis of the precise borders of Tollcross ('east along Lauriston as far as the former Royal Infirmary, with a sharp border in Lady Lawson Street, where K. Jackson's bar ...') which is in one sense completely bonkers, and yet also exactly the point. These cod-academic disputes about the precise meaning of neighbourhoods and placing of borders have obsessed citizens of every great city. Calder's notes are a watermark of authenticity. Yet he could not, either, have written these poems without a familiar, easy knowledge of Edinburgh's own poetic traditions. Robert Louis Stevenson and Norman MacCaig feature here directly, and there are sly references to many others – Robert Garioch's 'Embro' and the mist-shrouded, zany city of the scandalously under-rated Sydney Goodsir Smith. In a gleeful poem about curling, that ancient Embro ploy we find: 'Ice-capers! Time cannot stale/ our pot-bellied skittishness. Watch us/ frisking like penguins' and are transported back to the deeply affectionate, local mockery of Fergusson's eighteenth century. The greatest poetry is often like this, drawing on generations of observation, quoting and pushing forward. Forward: for Calder's Edinburgh is also today's, with its rattle-bag of races and voices, its pizzas and Tesco superstores. In the modern city, Calder displays his customary sharp, vivid observation and notes of pity, kindness and melancholy you don't find, for instance, in MacDiarmid. A special mention should be made of the concluding section, 'Horace in

Tollcross', because it so gloriously intertwines the sensibilities of materialistic, arrogant, energetic imperial Rome, and our own culture, 2000 years on. From Gavin Douglas's late-medieval remaking of Virgil, whose peasants devour bannocks and live under Scottish trees, to Garioch's glorious version of Guiseppe Belli's stinking, seething Rome, there has a been a particularly fine Scottish tradition of appropriation and well, it's a lot more than translation, as every reader of this book will soon discover, for Quintus Horatius Flaccus is as genial, coarse, witty and worldly patrolling the Edinburgh streets or leafing through the *Guardian*, as he ever was first time round. In one of the odes, Calder/ Horace says he believes 'I have fabricated verses/ which are, I hope, not contemptible,/ won't bubble and flit like foam.' He's right about that. This is a lovely book. If only every city in this land had a poet like him, what a richer country it would seem.

Andrew Marr
London, November 2004

One – Atmospherics

Small Game in Edinburgh Central

for Claire ('Urban') Fox

A grey mouse jumped out of my toaster –
three sleek inches, plus insolent little tail,
As he jinked off behind the Sugar Puffs,
I cried, 'I'll get you, bastard!'
Reached for my biggest knife. He squeaked in riposte:
'tee hee hee . . .
you'll never catch
me!'

At six a.m. I potter out for my paper.
Boss gull's on the doorstep jabbing at a binbag.
Backs to the middle of Spittal Street, rasps, 'After
you, squire...' Shrugs his black-wings, casually
casts a look round for rivals, over his shoulder . . .
'You all right then? We're running this street now.
See me right, we'll look after you.
OK?'

Passing the Links, I spot a grey squirrel
hoppiting hither and thither, much like
the hero of a demented Game Boy game.
I shout out, 'Some sensible places, people eat
rats with bushy tails like you.' He pipes back:
'Mistaken identity, mate. Me, I'm an innocent
forager. It's those red shites need cooking,
if you can find one nowadays – har, har, har.'

Disconcerted, I turn to my old friend Ma Pigeon
whose extended family graze Bread Street all day
much like archaeologists digging for Homeric
shards, and three thousand year old grains of barley.
'Don't worry, son,' she responds. 'See us – we're stable.
Shower us with carry-outs, we'll cope.
We're after a contract from Special Uplifts.
Excuse, please. I must just collect
that stray peanut.'

I am sure that not far, in Morningside and Dean,
urban foxes lurk, smirking. Edinburgh Central should be declared
a Game Park, and our new Parliament
should debate giving all fellow creatures the vote.
The gulls, I'm sure, support Rangers. As for the others,
Hibees or Jamboes, I don't care, they're us.
Me, I'm hereditary Dundee United
Wishing that cormorants too could flock to town.

By the Grassmarket

In February
near black midnight
a bold thrush chants
in that bare tree

Edinburgh Gulls

Riding inland on our peculiar winds
the gulls possess this city as of right.
They point blue sky, grey stone, with perfect white.

Pigeons who plod the pavements bickering
seem restive serfs under these lords of light,
finches mere flotsam of a moment's flickering.

Yet it's garbage gulls are after. Lower your sight
to spoiled, spilled binbags. A gull finds
fodder in squalor – so mean, so bright.

Talking to Mario Relich about Gulls in Edinburgh

The pigeons and gulls have taken over the town.
They are nesting here now (the gulls, I mean.)
The pigeons command all pavements, with their low brows
and determined strut, the boldest you've ever seen.
I like pigeons and gulls because they confirm
that life never stops changing. The scene
has been transformed by the pigeons and gulls
quite recently, taking over from the sparrows.
Nostalgic persons might talk as if life has been narrowed,
but I love the gulls, and the pigeons. They express
'nature' at its worst and its damned best,
refusing to stop pecking, refusing to die,
always prepared to give it another try
and (gulls, I mean) flying upwards towards the sun.

For Stephen Murray, regarding my city

As Venice, precisely –
Joe Losey noticed –
is the true city of Don Giovanni,
so Embro's the town
of Jekyll and Hyde
where the lofty discreetly pickle themselves in claret
while Brodie's gang exchange signals
in dark closes
and footpads and burkers lurk quite ready
to knock women and children down.
When mist blanks the streets,
power fails
and candles are lit in the bar
we know exactly where we are.

RLS

Beauty and fear: the long remembered faces,
childhood nightmares, far, far ago.
Wind clatters through the streets of Embro
with the devilish horseman whose demands we know
and the lost answers of the hollow places,
wind always asking what we owe, what we owe.

Biscuit and silk, bought skin from the Grassmarket,
whores blurted out at, far, far ago.
The devil inside the achieved person
goads the child of sorrow, acquainted with woe,
who puts queer questions to the smooth faces
of Embro professors, smart, so low.

Enormous Pacific, ocean skin wrinkling
beneath vast dawn – a long way to go
to meet new devils with their different masks,
cryptic creatures whether friend or foe,
flowered maidens with barely expressible graces,
where you dream of grey Embro, long, far ago.

To Honour Normanity

for Lynne Hainsworth

A statue of Norman MacCaig
with his lizard good looks
should stand on Bruntsfield Links:
at his feet, under
his shrewd sardonic gaze
a toad,
on his right arm, a falcon,
on his left palm, a dove . . .

(All to be sponsored, of course,
by a major distillery.)

Scott Monument

Like Castle Rock
taken for granted,
this stone thing created by hand.

A firtree
or a machine
imagined by Paolozzi?

A rocket
ready for launch
towards some Hibeejambo planet?

A focus
for many postcards
and home for the geist of a man.

Turkish Pepper

Antony, Rune and Joachin, my new Edinburgh neighbours –
such a thunder of benign and charming Norwegians
at your housewarming party
as a Scottish coast town could not, a thousand years back
have imagined! Viking favours
wakened me from illness and depression.
I gathered I'd read more sagas than some of them,
but I'd never imagined such a drink as Turkish Pepper –
sweet and strongly spirituous,
with a name connecting interesting regions,
far spice islands and Homer's Troy,
confirming my awed feeling, as a born-again boy
that your party was somehow epic.

For Lazio's

On the wall of my favourite restaurant
someone has painted a pastoral:
Italian donkeys, snowy Appennine mountains,
a hilltown, river and very old bridge.
There surely is a land of heart's desire.
The churlish and present world's excessively *méchant*,
but one should not fall over in face of it all.
Somewhere, not far away, there are clear fountains
impossible to bomb dead or set on fire,
and over the mountains, always another ridge.
The proprietor tells you it's where he comes from,
realistically set there on the wall.

Fin de Festival: Edinburgh 2000

Edinburgh rediscovers its classic grey –
most delicious of lourdness, an ecstasy of glum.
The trendy standups from London have been and come
and gone, and their posters remain to be torn down.
Yet echoes of Czech brass linger in the town,
wisps of luxurious violin,
and phantoms of airborne dancers tempt to sin
the time-preened matriarch who resumes her sway.

Echoes of Li He

Rabbie and his wenches
where are they sleeping?
Moonlight touches the dead palace
Thrushes sing all night.

Carriage like a bird's nest
horse like a hound
the ruined laird
called for claret in the tavern.

Moofies played under awnings
in a haar which reeks of flowers
On this long white day
don't count the pints we drink

O sun behind the Castle
stay behind the Castle
May one day be a thousand years
and never sink to rest.

Two – Light, Ice and Bars

Truth in Edinburgh, August 30

Truth is not like these fagends
I tip in the dustbin
from the car ashtray.
Truth's not smoked out.

Truth differs from this morning's
Scotsman, instant history –
truth didn't happen yesterday.

Nor is truth like the grey roofs
seen through my office window,
spires and castle clearcut against sky:

the city's thousands submerged
behind stone, beneath stone,
even the traffic at this height dumb.

Truth is a child
climbing the Mound in rain
Out of today into
tomorrow with effort.

September Starting

You think you could reach
across the Forth and touch
poppies in the Fife fields.

Roses appear huge as
cathedral windows.

Trees wear russet flecks
as if dressed up
for a night at the opera.

The light is so rich
with generous details

that a razory edge
of cold in the air
seems not so important.

Lothian

It would be the good childhood you never had.
The gold of sun and silver sea
that beckons deliciously out, the leaves of a tree
copper; on days which are never sad.

In imagination you have it as sun flares
on faces in Lothian Road this September,
shop girls and tourists – a childhood you remember
and never could have – no loneliness, no nightmare.

Greeting, Not Greeting

for Peta Sandars

To wake to the reassurance of grey stone streets
under a clouded, adequate Edinburgh sky,
finding one has the right change in one's pocket
for once: and for once there seems no cause to cry.
It is unnecessary to fly on a rocket.
Here is a day which one greets, not greeting.

Curling: Old Murrayfield Ice Rink

Ice-capers! Time cannot stale
our pot-bellied skittishness. Watch us
frisking like penguins who've guzzled
too many tunas
off Tristan da Cunha. But who
dares lampoon us? Directed
by skeely skips, we address
elementals with modest finesse.
Not 'bowls on the rocks' this, but stones
over ice: final realities.

Ice in captivity, certainly,
stones smoothed to human shining,
but heavy
real stones. See them sinuate
target-wards suavely.

Truly this joust has more import
than slim-shanked cavortings across there
by teeny-bopping, insouciant
easy
skaters.

Sweat, greybeards!
Concentrate. Sweep
hard, harder –
we might
yet
win.

Haymarket Sunset

for Sandy Robb

That lass in a woolly cap with earflaps
waiting at dusk for a bus by Haymarket Station
may conceivably have mince for brains
but at least her delicate profile and clear eyes
suggest potential. The young have not yet
been defeated, their gaze is towards tomorrow,
their step is forward. I stare back over decades –
so many times at this bus stop as sunset,
salmon and jade, has ebbed behind Corstorphine.
As I ride out once again to curling, my
tomorrows are fewer. However, week by week,
even hour by hour, Murrayfield ice is always
different. You have to adjust your weight,
your line, your sweep. And this light is always beautiful.

Elegy for a Curler

in memoriam, John Smith, d.2000

Not quite a straight takeout. Death curled it in,
somewhat, crab-wise. A strong stone was removed.
The metaphor breaks down. A stone is all thick skin.
The sensitive man who propelled it has been loved.
A stone, shoved out to the verge, is quite content
to hear no music, engage in no crack.
Another's vitality in the stone is spent.
It's the curler who feels fatal twinges in his back,
and the loss of his energies ripples as ice can't,
while somehow the curler's brief life sings
on, what the ageless stone can't hear. No stone ever
counted the stones at rest in the rings
and called 'Sweep! Sweep!' No stone's that clever,
but the curler who watched how the stone on the ice bends
gathered all from life that he could snatch –
tall children, and farewell from many friends.
Death's grabbed one end, but hasnae won the match.

Armistice Day

The high gold leaves arc down
but on bushes some green ones tease
a wind which will grow colder.

In this playpark children pick
crooked ways, run crashingly
on the climbing ensemble, intending
whatever it is they fancy. The tallest boy
walks up the short slide, the smallest girl
makes meshed ropes her munro.
Everything's so safe, you'd think they wouldn't bother.

Yet as energy pleases itself, stories
must mutter through their minds.
Life matters for them as much perhaps
as it ever will.

Once the squaddies ripped in Flanders
and the desert's cindered tankcrews
raided nests, chased footballs,
hung on trees as small
heroes.
       Worse stories came true
than they could have fancied when kek-
kek-kek-you're-dead they gunned
their sisters down with sticks
and trampled chrysanthemums.

In the bleached blue sky
a cloud like a deity's hand
quenches the sun.
But releases it. My four year-old
makes a see-saw go single-handed. The tot
with a ball in proportion like Atlas's globe
might one day sidefoot such a thing into goal
and jubilate under November sun.

The rest go. My boy with the freedom of the frame
tells himself stories. May some perhaps
which are good come true. May the worst of his life
not be bombardment and may insane Achilles
never come upon him
near a city soon to be burnt and sacked
unarmed beside Xanthos cutting wood.

For Rupsha Fraser on her eighteenth birthday

Today, by offhand miracle, is a treat
of November summer when the tipsy
spectres of Pakistani cricketers dance
over sculpted leaves of maple, golden
chestnut. All collapsed Augusts now
project on morningside the frail faraway
sexuality of Maurice Ravel.

There is a pizza to be constructed
on the stonebake of the sun from filligree
of falling, twirling daydreams. Could one solidify
dark rum breath from Guyana jungle, place it
beside petrified shards of frozen
Finnish water to configure
a terrain of rainforest trees and tundra where
the douanier's elegant beasts minuet

with Saint Nicholas and his altogether elsewhere
reindeer? Dance, love,
upon a margharita of Inverness
and Ganges delta, with prancing tiger
from greenbrown sunrise until the pale Basque moon
calls Mother Goose's children to their beds.
Rupsha, here's music for you, as the leaves fall
through this uncanny perfect blue

armistice of November Embro day –
may your bare feet as they dance never strike a splinter.

Meeting Mike Jannetta and Andy Ross at Una's party: December 1998

Sudden
to see you again.
How many years?
Smack
of stones curling to kiss
on ice, whenever.

Arandora Star
drops through the sea.
Missiles cruise on Saddam.
Our collie seeks sheep to control
running mad
through Baghdad.

On TV politicos lie.
On granite, our pavings,
pigeons bicker.
This year, in Princes Street Gardens,
on ice, polished stone
rumbles to target.

Vibrating coldness
as a stone curls
under the Castle.
Camped homeless on Tollcross paving,
that boy, what's his name?
He replies: 'David Livingstone.'

We should remember
the beauty of this room –
December's level sunlight,
wine with a view to the Pentlands,
along with everything else
we should not be forgetting.

Salutations

at the Scottish National War Memorial – for Caroline Scott

Why, after the volcanoes, did we arrive here?
Schemies, what was the scheme?
Why were we born here, addicts of beer and whisky,
in a country where it's really too cold for sex
and glacial Calvin makes us feel guilty
if, by some odd fluke, it happens? Where wifies
chat endlessly about the price
of scones in Thomson's of Dumbarton?
What directed that vaulting
vision of ourselves which has littered
our bones from St Lucia to Madagascar,
Chile to Kamchatka?
Maybe some answers are here
where the names of our courageous dead
are preserved in a sanctuary
where sculptures honour also canaries and camels
who worked with us for their own reasons,
in Hell, in torrid seasons,
perhaps because they liked the wee smiles
of hard-boozing Spartans in tartan,
or perhaps they had some consciousness of Margaret,
the Saint who gave people and dumb beasts wells.

Thinking about Derek Walcott

for Pat Byer

When a woman you care about
throws strong cider at you,
you realise some end of the world has been reached,
and we might as well call it Morningside, where
on Sunday the veteran lady, impeccably clad,
after Kirk hovers into Safeways,
and the checkout lass kens exactly
to sell her discreetly her half bottle of voddy
so that all the afternoon she can sit
in her stench of lavender and polish
to brood over what she has loved and lost,
and lost by not sufficiently loving.
Such a character, like Helen's, should not be impeached.
She travels with us, the perpetual wild rovers.

Dawn Walk Downhill in Spring

One's aim might be
to make a poem
out of every pavingstone
from Bruntsfield via Tollcross
to the Usher Hall,

to annotate any random gull
which shrieks at dawn,

to evoke the face of each
early-morning-out-and-about
careworn woman,

and write elegiac haikus
about individual daffodils.

In practice, our lives being not much longer
than a gutter pigeon's,
one can only reiterate large
simplicities –

blue sky, mild wind, grey stone
in a mobile shining world:
self not alone.

Sandy Bell's

There was a Bell
who was Sandy, had
Embro relations.

Now the bar's relations
are with any place –
Kansas, Bulgaria –

where Burns is known
and fiddle understood.

What rivers of music
have flowed from this well.

Staffordshire Terrier in the Auld Clachan

This dog from the Black Country whimpers,
though his owner assures me
that he's 'at home in the bar'.
He's black and squat and you might
suppose he is unhappy
when he jumps up – perpendicular – and licks men's faces.
His pantings suggest appetites
that range far further than this lino floor.
What pits, by which potteries, might be his favourite places?
He grumbles, dozes, growls
and snaps at people's trousers.
I like his face.
It reminds me of my father,
a gentle person, sometimes frustrated.

Dapper the Day

Out of the lurcher darkness, black country
comes such beauty –
this dog in the bar in Bread Street, for instance
and the lassie
the barman lounges to the door each day to see,
just her black loveliness going to the bus stop
out of Africa, Ghana,
always something new –
looking dapper the day,
seriously gorgeous,
has travelled further than epic Zwangendaba
to match the misunderstood lovely
black dog and the friendly
gloved ghost of Randolph Turpin.

Surnames

for Rodney Relax

The friendliness of the world
in this fine April
resumes with sunniness and crack about surnames.
It is as if the accident
of being half-McKail
or semi-Graham
makes human and able
to talk to each other all
Jean and indeed *Jean-Jacques* Tamson's bairns.
So that Rodney underpaid in that kitchen
and the high class Embro dominatrice
I met by accident just now
are related like my favourite Icelandic grannie
each to each and to all the transitory stars.

Three – Affections

Three Plaints of Hamish McIlwraith

April Folly

If I mistake the pager in my pocket
for a spring songbird, darling, don't give me a rocket.
This is a strange season. The other night it snowed
in mid-April, an inch on the cars parked in my road,
but on the bushes like blossom. Then came rain
as raw as November. Since what's real is bizarre –
here in Edinburgh, at least – now that the sun is back
I adjure myself never to doubt your truth again.
Through astounding nature, you are just what you are.
Beyond prediction, I learn from you what I lack.

Homing North to Edinburgh

I ride in a kind of cold fever
with a train ticket out of brick Suffolk
where white may on hedge is in fever.

I ache as a man who may never
be nursed by what he desires –
your voice and silk person forever.

Self cure is my soundest endeavour
My city of stone will soon hold me,
where leafing resembles endeavour.

Yet stone cannot cool a cold fever
nor spring fail to stir gorse in Scotland
– reviving or curing my fever

despite or through my endeavour,
your absence or loving forever,
or rather till death stills all fever.

May Winds

Fickle Eros picks his time to strike –
Edinburgh freezes greyly in May and it's over.
My prophetic soul forewarned me in the chill wind.
Then you phoned and told me you'd picked another lover.

'Easy come, easy go?' Not easy and not gone
You sounded notes in me never heard before.
Happiness never was the point, perhaps.
Mainly, it mattered that life meant more.

You came like a slow wind. Are you gone with the wind?
Fidelity and betrayal are faint specks
compared to the mountains, the sky and the wind of love
which surges and blurts and doesn't care what it wrecks.

Do I bin you as a folly, return to despair,
or settle sanely for life which means less?
No. I am grateful. I can't just wince and shrug.
I desire to weep, and yet I want to bless.

Sequence in Cold Spring: Distances, Closeness

Long Distance

Only now do I realise
how much I had come to need you,
to talk about snow
or that very special mist
which completely obscured the Castle last night
and somehow, as with a dress and a body, revealed it.
I wish I could write better verses to read you
down long distance phone
about that mist and wherever it's gone.

Migrations

Amidst the dredge of accents
and the din of jukebox
your voice repeatedly returns
as something which yearns beyond Birmingham,
enters north of Ibrox,
has a name past Cornwall,
ships coal further than Cardiff,
remains part of Scotlandesh
and Morningside
but wider – strong cider.
You could airfreight that sound
as far as Carolina
or the Blue Ridge Mountains of Virginia,
dear love, to converse with Laurel and Hardy.

Skating in Bahrain

You speak it long distance,
a phrase which delights me
about a reality.
Rich people live in that place
without nationality,
Marks and Sparks,
you tell me, open a shop there next week.
So why shouldn't there be an occasional curling Greek?

Writing as a Small Connoisseur of Pizza

The worlds one has gained,
the worlds one has lost,
the corners I've turned,
the coins that I've tossed,
must not all dissolve
like mist
or the ash of the fags that I've burned
getting pissed
before you've returned.
Dario's Pizza del Mare – I
respect gamberetti,
don't charge through the vino,
regain my resolve,
re-encounter the sky,
meet light snow like confetti
wherever you've been, oh.

News for you of the Corries

Down in the Street
there is little rapture
and much bad happening.
Deirdre, Mike and Ken
carry on and on
amid dreadful ruptures
and bits of battering.
But the sense of sweet
Rover's Return meeting lingers,
of women's and men's
embracing fingers,
in the street which is never gone,
where we all drop in
from time, in time.

Bread Street

Is also the street of naan
and pizza
and posho.
Its name represents where
people meet,
that promenade
of Scotlandesh,
where we must andare al spasso,
person with person,
you and me, dear,
under whatever sun.

Just Off Lothian Road

Weekends the theatres debouch their crowds
in Grindlay Street, in Cambridge Street

Hibees and Jamboes raise their slurry chants
in West Port, in Bread Street

Alone in bed I listen to the sounds
of life outside, in Spittal Street

Imagination takes me far away
to Lawley Road, to Miguel Street.

You're Coming Back

It is your coming back which now concerns me –
how, after absence in the Gulf's glare, will you perceive my
features faded by our snell north winds?

These streets persist and you have been at home with
our blown-about litter of chip papers, rattling cans,
the black binbags squatting by our doorways.

Surely the Castle will remain for you
what it always has been? While my body decays,
these grey stones hang invincibly above us.

Somehow or other, this city, yours by birth,
mine by choice, will still contain us both. Surely
we cannot cease to have this much in common?

As for my snotters, my arthritis and my bad teeth
you have formerly in your charity forgiven these.

Four – Horace in Tollcross

Horace in Tollcross

Eftir some odes of QH Flaccus

This is a sequence of updatings of Odes by Horace (Quintus Horatius Flaccus), who died in in his fifties in 8 BC, just before the start of our first 'millennium'. The son of a freed slave who held a minor official post in a southern province of the Roman domains, Horace, despite the indiscretion of bearing arms for Brutus and Cassius at Phillipi, attracted the mighty patronage of Maecenas, friend of the first Emperor, Augustus. He flattered both of them, but inveighed against big landowners, corrupt businessmen and politicians and Rome's wealthiest classes in general. His ironic attitudes towards politics and society remain attractive, as does his delight in wine, but, while his bisexuality is tolerable these days, erotic capers with very young slaves are hardly in order. So I have updated Horace completely to present-day Edinburgh, two-thousand plus years later, trying to imitate the quirky trajectories of thought and feeling which make his Odes so companionable.

1.1 Maecenas atavis edite regibus . . .

Consider, Kenneth, best teacher, my inveterate
staunch friend, still, in your nineties, sprightly –
after torturous training, the distance runner
breasts the Olympic tape close to collapse,
then, highest on the podium, during his anthem,
glares like a king at massed cameras, anointed.
The jovial Member elected again, third time,
jubilates over his own immortal virtue.
Friend Sid imagines when his shares romp skywards
that he deserves the earth he believes he owns.
The joiner content with his own competence,
and skilling his son, wouldn't work on the oil rigs
for ten times his current income, using brawn
he has no desire at all to develop. Salesmen
stalled in mid-journey when the scheduled
express is cancelled, curse the wandering life,
yearn for their gardens and quiet crack in the local,
yet still, shunning the benefit queue, keep moving.
Your lounger stocked up with bargain Chilean plonk
passes whole afternoons sipping in front of the telly
or daydreams, half-snoozing, in a deserted park,
yet his neighbour's mad keen on TA – watch me: Rambo! –
and fantasises about cacophonous wars
merest thought of which makes his mother shudder.
The midsummer fisherman keeps vigil all night
by a mountain burn, spurning his young bride's bed
for the twitch of a bite, thrill of a sudden, shining
catch. And for my part, away with the fairies,
I care for nothing beyond these rapt moments

when Time is somewhere else and my verses find
swift channels through life's rocks. If you approve
of my efforts to touch the turn-ups (as it were)
of MacDiarmid's trousers, can find a line of mine
to set beside your favourite Keats and Owen, then
my stride will be light again, my greying head
will dance like a teenager's among the stars.

1.5   Quis multa gracilis te puer in rosa . . .

What presentable lad with a whiff about him
of best aftershave now upon your fragrant double
    bed pleasures you, wrigglesome Sadie? What
    sucker just now believes he has bagged

your warm-seeming smile? Soon he will be cursing
the bad luck which threw you together, will retch as tempests
    hurl forty-foot waves across
    the ocean he thought was a delectable lake –

hang on, though, poor fellow, still deluded he's won
for keeps a prize inamorata, the 'love
    of his life'. But your wind will always veer
    as it damn well likes. Any bloke who embarks

on that seductive blue's cast away. One old buffer
whose photo new lovers might just find in your cupboard
    paddled for dear life to shore, then blessed
    the solidity of mud, and was snug without you.

1.8 Lydia, dic, per omnis . . .

Monica, lass, tell us –
(swearing by Big Tam and God Almighty) – how
    you have so wasted by sex
an excellent cricketer, someone who should be
    in the winter nets very next Tuesday?
Why is the Dougie we know no longer found
    among his mates in the boozer,
watching England's latest collapse on the telly?
    Why did he not view with us
Man United going down to Vasco Da Gama?
    Why does he steal himself away
from the veteran bruisers, the boys, and languish
    in thrall to you, the lass?
Reveal what ploys will get him back to us,
    darling, because we need him
to turn his arm over for us and bat.

1.9 Vides ut alta stet nive candidum . . .

See how the bright snow has drenched the Pentlands now
wifies skid in Lothian Road before sludge freezes
    and frost makes merest perambulation harder
    still as icy gales assault the air.

I'll rebuff the December cold, turn up all heaters.
Now, dear young Stewart, pray visit and bring in with you
    whatever fifteen-year-old Glenlivet Vic
    Wine's got on special offer. Then don't stint:

four fingers! Let polis and weathermen fret. Some time
this collieshangie of tempests will exhaust itself,
    rowans will quiver to rest in Embro gardens
    and elderly sycamores cease their shaking.

Don't let thoughts of unthinkable future bug you.
Every tomorrow is bonus – you not being dead
    or crippled, yet – so try to feel grateful
    for that, and since you remain supple,

your age short of middle, you might consider raving
the night away. Now, after midnight's the best time
    for wholly unsubtle propositions muttered
    over the disco's unrelenting beat –

then her place for top-up vodka and maybe, maybe,
the lass won't be so utterly sick blootered
    that she'll fall into snoring without first
    at least removing her warm, damp knickers.

1.11   Tu ne quaesieris, scire nefas, quem mihi, quem tibi . . .

Not you dear, nor me, can forecast even in
general what will befall us. We must thole
what tabloid soothsayers cannot predict.
We can't deflect gales which will batter Argyll
and shake Embro slates. Over our coffee, now,
nasty time hurdles fast. Life's short. Keep cool. Don't
expect chocolate fudgecake with cream every morning.
Carpe diem. Enjoy this delicious biscuit.

1:13   Cum tu, Lydia, Telephi . . .

Monica, when you Alas
-tair this, Alastair that... 'His
    hips are so slim, chin's
so gorgeous,' I wince. Glance at my envious
    (unlike his) pale lips.
My brain blanks out when I try
    to imagine your hots
for this identikit action man, and
    if one of your boozy wrassles
has left scars on your velveteen shoulders,
    biffs on your bosom, that
scalds me. But listen, my honey, this
    chancer won't last long, this brute
whose kisses bruise your luscious mouth,
    vector of nectar. Face
up to this – the best relationship
    is steady affection, staying
pals without rumpusses: maybe no
    shagging at last, but at least
still closely in touch on your dying day.

1.16   O matre pulchra . . .

Most gracious woman with abundant talents
if you still have the nasty verses which
　　once, outraged, I uttered against you,
　　　　flush them, now, down the cludgie.

Not Jimmy Hendrix at his most dementing,
not Shostakovich screaming indiscretions,
　　nor hugest rolled-up spliffs of cannabis,
　　　　massed Carnival steel drums

take a man over like bitter jealous anger,
so that even our wildest Tollcross weather
　　when the west gale whirligigs, full binbags
　　　　dance and second-floor windows

are assailed by chip-pokes, can't stall it, at all.
Curse this – in our make-ups wrath's part of
　　of what keeps us going, we are still
　　　　furclad feart mammoth-hunters.

Reckless wrath destroyed that miraculous
Moorish civility of fertile Andalucia,
　　crushed the architect Incas, leaving
　　　　Macchu Picchu to the condors,

extinguished harm-free Guanches and Tasmanians –
please, dear, be pacified, it was the mad
　　writhings of bare forked animal which forced
　　　　brutish jibes out of my sad

rancid consciousness. If you can now consent
to disregard my shabbiness and accept
   this apology, poor even of its kind, might
    we meet again, friends?

1.25   Parcius iunctas quatiunt fenestras

Young rugby-players don't now so often
rap on your windows, do they, Monica?
Your door, once almost revolving with traffic,
   cleaves to its sill.

Your beauty sleep's safe now, not as in those
mad days when all night randy three-quarters
wailed 'Monica, let me in, I must see you,
   or die here'.

Soon you'll be drinking solo, never receiving
a newcomer's second glance. You'll pace
the New Town homewards alone on black nights
   when east wind

rages like your own raddled libido, that lust
which whips veteran lionesses and bitches.
You'll mutter to yourself about how ungraciously
   these kids

go for the juicy brainless bimboes
or hot discontented young wives, while
experienced shags rattle along granite pavements
   like autumn leaves.

1.26   Musis amicus tristitiam et metus . . .

Horace being just now my mucker, I dismiss
headcold and debts. They can ramble
   to wherever they damn well like
      beyond furthest Hebrides.

Happy for a wee whilie not to be battered
by worries about which bullyboy despotism
   might soon be about to reproduce
      horrific headlines, what scandal

will next assail the London Home Office, I
ply my pen. Excellent old QH Flaccus
   to whom the nine muses were dear and almost
      literal, since you'd lived in Greece,

assist me to imagine in midwinter
summer blossoms for dearest Celia.
   You can help me present to her
      the sweet notoriety she deserves,

and with the entire tradition of verse
which you and our brother Jack Mapanje
   and so many others represent
      praise her in a fresh whole voice.

1.27   Natis in usum laetitiae scyphis . . .

To set up a rammy over whisky and beer
is what keelies in Galashiels do – atavism
      to be redcarded. Revered John Barleycorn
      deserves better than daft stushies.

A comfortable café-bar just isn't the place for
see-you-ootside-Jimmies. Wheesht, wheesht:
      Cool it, mates. Your elbows
      should remain steady to lift full pints.

Yes, OK, I myself am eftir getting properly
pished. But just now I want quiet to listen to
      what our mucker Sandy may divulge
      about this new bird he reckons he's found.

Out with it, don't back off, or I won't accept
your offer of another pint. After all she
      must be quite something to have attracted
      someone of your famously fastidious

taste. Just tell us the whole romantic story now –
we won't clype aboot it outside these four... WHAT!!!
      Matie, you're doomed. That whure will have
      your testicles for earrings. Surely YOU

could've done better than THAT... But it's no use.
Jock Stein himself couldn't coach you out of
      that creature's crafty clutches. Even my doughty
      Muse, I confess, is completely helpless.

1.31 Quid dedicatum poscit Apollinem? . . .

What boon, Ogun, can I quasi-priest-like,
your poet, observing you in my personal
   shrine across my living room, request?
     Not might-be-windfall shares

in NatWest, not a stake in novelty Internet
commerce, nor an HSBC get-rich-slow
   account, nor even fertile acres snaffled
     up now all farms are in crisis –

no, let the dodgy GM entrepreneurs fash
themselves, and I won't grudge wee chancers
   their electronic stock-market gambles
     nor salesmen huge weekend swallies,

which they must deserve, doing Formula One
speeds up and down the M9, poor fellows,
   risking their licences. As for myself,
     I'll settle for mango-juice and cheddar

(with lime pickle). Ogun, mate, all I ask
is stamina to go swimming, to relish our
   daft Tollcross life – and, as mind crumbles,
     some persisting tact with metre.

1.38   Persicos odi . . .

Lass, I hate Glasgow novelties –
cute hairstyles bore me
rinsed with weird dyes. I don't care
for the latest hit singles.

Nothing beats au naturel,
even with dandruff. Buy me
strong beer and our greyshot locks
will seem amply radiant.

2.14   Eheu fugaces, Postume, Postume . . .

Oh damn, how they whizz past, Glenday, Glenday,
irresistible years! Hairloss and arthritis, then
    senectude, death, which no one can beat.
    Fitness classes can't stall their roll

onwards, no pal, if you donated ten thousand
pounds a year to Cancer Research or bought
    the flashiest private healthcare, still
    you'd pass into the dark darkness where

every one of us trousered or skirted animals
who've relished tasty morsels and sunny days
    must end, whether we're suited executives
    or dolequeue shufflers bumming fags.

It was no use our being too young for National Service
and not getting trapped on the stands at Hillsborough,
    missing out on TB and polio
    and somehow avoiding AIDS – we born goners

must at last confront whatever Ivan Ilyich at
last thought he saw, or watch, as so often's been rumoured,
    phantasmagoria of our entire lives
    flash profitlessly past in seconds.

So goodbye coffee and cake in Filmhouse, jolly cuddles
under warm blankets. Of all those pleasures foreseen
    in easeful retirement, only the blankness
    of deepest sleep might conceivably linger.

Your inheritors will flog off all your favourite CDs,
maybe read some of your books you never got round to,
    and likely splash out some of your legacy
    on better parties than you've ever hosted.

2.15   Iam pauca aratro iugera regiae . . .

Soon, I foresee, all the cornershops will go under
crushed by the chains fastened by megamoney.
    With sparrowhead sales staff lounging bored,
    book superstores will outglare city lights.

Once scholarly codgers yarned about their shelves
where editions published decades before still peeked
    – ignorance, now, is insouciant about prices
    which then provided small dealers canny margins

when little lefty presses stood some kind of chance
and a slightly-nicked cover could get you a nifty discount.
    Johnson would have detested these glitzy mazes
    of glib fiction and coffee-table inanities.

In my far youth, we valued public ownership.
and private wealth conducted itself discreetly.
    Now it's consume! in yer face, consume!
    Entrepreneurs ettle to bottle the rain.

No one back then dared dispraise engine drivers – mighty,
those gods who commanded our trains: and public libraries
    were cherished like Pallas Athene's temples,
    which, for us, in effect, they were.

2.16   Otium divos rogat in patenti

The traveller hopes for calm heavens, no turbulence
juddering the Boeing, no floods or blizzards
to interrupt his taxi's reliable progress
to a sound hotel,

and peace is what unwashed, shell-shocked Chechens
and Congolese guerrillas camped in the bush
must surely yearn for, beatitude which oil-riches,
Brian, can't buy.

A charge by mounted polis, or water cannon,
can briskly disperse a mob of football casuals
but not those louts of the mind, brute thoughts crowding
the dark bedroom.

You're OK, live well, if you can make good soup,
buy fresh bread, then eat off clean plates on an easy
chair, so long as you've no panic or envy,
just comfy hopes.

Why drive over the limit when Time will cancel all trips?
Why hanker after patios by blue pools
in sunny faraways? What tanned exile ever escaped
home thoughts?

Panic, that pox, jeers on the wings of the Boeing,
out-paces the Derby-winner and the Mercedes,
rushes wildly outstripping any cloud-hurtling
North-Westerly gale.

To be happy now, careless about next Monday,
enjoy all possible jokes, is the one way to blunt
life's vicious macheté. 'Nobody's perfect',
as Joe E. Brown put it.

Lengthy senectude wasted Harold Wilson,
Death cut Martin Luther King down at his summit,
and any day now may bar you from basic goods
still lavished on me.

You've got your three GTs and natty runabout,
your castle in Spain, *pied-à-terre* in the Seychelles,
designer jerseys, lobster for lunch at command
and the latest immaculate

hi-fi – but I'm wealthy also. My patroness Luck
(decent lass) gives me a central ground floor flat,
an ear for Bach and Mozart, and no jealous thoughts
about jackpot winners.

3.1 Odi profanum vulgus et arceo . . .

I turn my back on suckers who can credit
Guardian G2, or wallow in *Hello*, to
push fresh verse towards the uncluttered minds
of witty schoolkids, independent wifies.

Blairite heid-yins may control many dupes
and playdoh creatures, but their existences
remain midge-brief as ours within millions
of years amidst the millions of stars.

Some guy creates a super swimming pool
bigger than next-door's. It rains all summer.
On the election trail three candidates
set out: one believes that his wealth

will see him through, another his reputation
as incorruptible, and the third his faction's
tight organisation – yet it's still as if in
the Lottery machine the balls go round.

When criminal investigation hovers
over Kohl or Archer, how can they savour
the best gourmet food? Such men, no music
soothes and Tyson-strong sleeping pills

are needed to knock fear out, yet an odd-jobbing
part-time fisherman in a highland village
slumbers fine amid the agreeable
cries of birds and the wind's soft sigh.

Rough seas outside can't agitate under blankets
a person who's content and warm, nor even
the lashing gales of February bashing
windows, when floody puddles surge over

football pitches, then freeze, so that key matches
are called off and administrators caught
on the hop (again!) try to pin entire blame on
the Met Office and Heather the Weather.

Now Tesco drives yet another superstore
into green fields, robbing birds and rodents
of trees, hedges, ditches, in hope that share –
holders can gorge still more profits, yet

horrible thoughts take the lift to the highest penthouse,
sit in the back of the most extravagant limo.
When private jets set out for very enchanting
island Edens, forebodings yammer inside them.

Can fanciest clothes designed by the likes of
Versace or the plushest of new carpetting
hoover up care, or the priciest champagne
and perfume tame the pangs of cancer?

Why dream of a second-home mansion which might
cut you off from your mates (See him! – the sell-out . . .)
when all I lust for – north or west of Perth –
is a smallish retreat with studio and mod cons?

3.9   Donec gratus eram tibi . . .

Just listen to what
a bardie's slick tongue on occasion can somehow
    contrive, as I report –
'Oh, magnificent Monica, momentously lickerish

    lovely, when you affirmed
that you craved me, I was Desperate Dan in Pieland.'
    'Sure, Andy, while
you amused yourself by describing my mighty tits

    as your muse, I was
beguiled, but . . .' 'Yes, clever Sally's my lass now,
    the harpist from Lewis.
I'd tackle Mike Tyson to spare her harrassment.'

    'OK, then, brilliant Bruce,
kilted heir to Muck Castle, fancies me to bits,
    and I, too, him.
I'd nurse him for months through the foulest lurgi.'

    'Yeah . . . but suppose
you-me got together again? Come on, imagine
    I gave Sal the shove
and Brucie spurned your grovelling adoration?'

    'Though he's star-class
and you're an unpunctual heidbanging scruff –
    Oh well, I guess
I might just bear you, care for you, better and worse.'

3.21 O nata mecum consule Manlio . . .

Fifteen year old whisky, created
same year I moved to Tollcross, loosener
   of lyrics, libidinous madness and argie-
    bargies, then – thanks pal – slumber;

precious old Islay, saved up for some special
occasion, let's forget all conjectures, for this
   is it, your time is now. My guest wistfully
    wishes to sip something better than blended.

He's a philosopher, mind you, high
on such as Heidegger, Habermas, yet
   he'll appreciate you, just as Davie Hume
    maintained his serenity with claret.

Dram, in your spirited race you outpace
brains sluggish as mine: but the real thinker
   runs with his deepest and most periculous
    fancies as John Barleycorn cheers him on.

Creature, you bring hope to shoo off worries –
could give the embattled poor courage.
   Bureaucrats might ettle to bugger them
    up, but after some swigs they'd rally.

It's so good to sit up late, with women
whose faces seem to unwrinkle, hips lighten
   as golden malt brightens lips and laughter
    till dawn vaults over Arthur's Seat.

3.30   Exegi monumentum . . .

Much tougher than Teflon, towering above
the Millennium Dome, my swift scribblings,
love, have jointed you and me in structures
north-easters can't knock over, nor can
the death-watch-beetle-tick of years nibbling
centuries wholly devour our names. Spooks
of us will survive crematoria. While the future
Internet prognosticates final disasters,
on it, my fame will gather moss, though rolling.
Where the Water of Leith slinks, where once,
over clarty causeways, Jamie Saxt ruled
a truculent people, I will be remembered
as a maut-heid who crafted lyrics, not unaware of
Castalian tradition. Be chuffed, my dear,
since you fully deserve our posterity of acclaim
– and treat me just now to one of Zamzamah's curries.

4.7 Diffugere nives . . .

Snow's pissed off and our wan northeastern green
peeps out on the Meadows' trees, as, greatly daring
daffodils venture warily. Now Leith's Water
threatens no terraces with spate. Woollies
cast off, voices of lovely students trill
more perkily, and as Frisbies fly
bosoms bounce cheerfully over the churned mud..
But don't kid yourself. That, mate, is twelve months more
kaput, and every day-devouring hour
reports, 'You'll never have time to re-read
all the Waverley novels, fathom Stevens or trip
to far Samoa. Your clogs, if you've still got legs,
will pretty soon be popped.' Grey May
might become tepid, July be OK, then autumn
will flatter us with Timon's gold – however,
lashing cold will be back and your Power Cards
will soon be expiring Christie-quick. Frigorific
North Sea repairs itself endlessly, but we
will pronto like Branson and Dewar, even Big Tam,
be smoke above crematoria. And who knows
if a meteor won't end life on earth anyway? (Boom!)
Coddle yourself right now. Your heirs should expect nothing
once ants traipse over your ashes, and furthermore,
after the obits have connived in your misdeeds,
your excellent genes and your petty kindnesses
won't like a Switchcard swipe you back into sunshine.
Mighty have Kennedys been, and charming was John,
but into the ocean he dropped like a lead shot.
Diana was breenging with wealth and the hots
when a pickled chauffeur careered her towards Lethe.

4.8   Donarem pateras grataque commodus . . .

Truly, I'd like to proffer presents
to all my friends – fine pottery,
CDs at whim, even antique videos
of Scotland's Grand Slams. Willie Prosser,
assuming that I owned numerous
Paolozzis, shimmering landscapes
by Rob Maclaurin – now, there's two
absolute artists – you could choose
the pick of my collection. But
I'm broke, and you've probably got
all the pictures you need, and as
for poems, plenty you love, yet
that's all, immodestly, I reckon
I can give to people, not inert
heirloom thingies. Bland memorials
brought home no abiding glory
for such warriors as Abercrombie
(who he?). Fighting Mac captured
hearts of historians, and a poet.
Eloquent bardies, in prose, damned
Earl Haig (unfairly – maybe) and
frankly no-one would remember
your mighty predecessor Erskine
if Rabbie hadn't rhymed for him,
while as for Wallace, old Blind
Harry, surely, invented the bloke?
Power to make one flighty lass
into Highland Mary, give Aberfeldy

glamour to match Tivoli, rides
on the poet's tongue. Our Muse
won't let merit perish and can make
wee nutters immortal. Thanks to her
John Maclean down the Broomielaw
proceeds aye-wise, vigorous song
reversed in all human sympathy dark
Culloden's defeat, RLS hunts on
home from the hill, and the Drunk
Man prophesies all that we might yet be.

4.9   Ne forte credas interitura . . .

Over the secret river which flows underground
down from Tollcross, I have fabricated verses
   which are, I hope, not contemptible,
      won't bubble and flit like foam.

True, Burns and MacDiarmid were certainly better –
but Mark Alexander Boyd penned one wee cracker,
   Robert Garioch crafted stuffy pieces,
      and Violet Jacob haunting verses,

nor have the bairn's-rhymes of RLS and Soutar
melted like candy-floss into toom oblivion.
   Of many mighty, passionate stanzas
      set to fiddle or pipe tunes, we've

forgotten the authors' names, but never the words.
Do you think Helen of Sparta was unique
   in falling for a dressy chancer who
      sallied at her with princely manners?

Was Johnny Armstrong the first kenspeckle reiver?
Were there no lairdies bonnier than Moray?
   Was Flodden really worse than Pinkie,
      Dundee the only corpse at Killiecrankie?

Singers have served some with words, the residue
have dithered unweepably into the dark darkness.
   When prowess is not catchily celebrated
      it's little better than those hushed-up shames

which families burn with old letters, or doomed Charges
of various Heavy Brigades, no doubt, which never
    attracted a skeely versifier's alert
      attention. Be sung – or be forgotten.

Tommy, you should not be left without fame in verse.
May you be rhymed with Red John Maclean of the Clyde,
    lest you be lost in sneeze-making archives
      of brown newsprint, or Net's unfrequented crannies.

You, who denounce the greedy and all those comfy
who even unwittingly cheesegrate the old and sick,
    meanwhile, for yourself, unattracted by any mansion
      ringed with high fences, security alarms,

I hail you, not as a May the Twelfth freak wonder,
but hero of every day when you arraign
    evasive Blairclones, hugger-mugger quangoes,
      bribed accountants and venal journos,

evoke for judges Justice above their quibbles, thrust
big issues into well-foddered faces, summon
    to demonstrate for themselves the poor who
      are richer in kindness than bankers, better friends, so

there's truer happiness for the man who detests
compromise more than prison, pinches no pennies,
    insists on generosity. I implore you –
      Haud Forrit! Never let up!

4.12   Iam veris comites, quae mare temperant . . .

Now April's amiable sou-westerly
ripples new leaves and blossoms, weeds
assert themselves and Forth and Tay
    flush Highland snow away.

Hear how those non-erogenous, pretty
tits chirp in their nests, while raucous
gulls wax maternal and wagtails flitter
    hitherly, thitherly.

Out on the Meadows, Oz backpackers pluck
guitars, watch tentative cricketers. My statuette
of dark Ogun, touched by sudden sunshine,
    looks minded to join them.

The season calls for an al fresco party,
but if you, Janet, award-winning peeress
of mega-Creators, accept my invitation,
    recall that all other poets are still

flat broke, so bring with you some up-market
winebox, that we may freely – only towards
the point where credit-card debts are ignored –
    inventively orgy.

Come all ye, bardies, but don't imagine
I've some polished cabinet clash-packed with
gin, brandy, Babycham, schnapps, etcetera –
    just cans in the fridge.

Forget rejection slips and misprints, but let's
remember the dark darkness we're heading for
as we revel in jests and perceptions, tipsy
   in this delicious blink.

Envoi

Sabine

for Rex Taylor

Morning star. Dawn in Dumfriesshire,
Haiku – an owl hoots
over the mill stream.

This millhouse recrafted
less like Thor Ballylee
than Horace's farm.

Firstlight glows in the crimson cheek
of a pheasant browsing
your bird tray.

Under patterns of black twigs
against lucid sky,
November primroses.

Doves flit from your multiplex cot
where they nest
above white geese, pert mallards.

May your racked wines please you
long among leaves' goldfall,
goosesquawk and dovesong.

Notes

General

When I first visited Edinburgh around 1960, to take in the Festival, I stayed in a B&B in Polwarth. Thereafter, my parent's flat on Queensferry Street at the West End was my base. A permanent move here in 1971 soon took me just across the Dean Bridge to Queensferry Road. A few years later, I commuted in awhile from West Lothian. Then I sojourned in Marchmont, that patch of Frenchified or Flemified late-nineteenth century architecture south of the Meadows, a base for yah students and Inspector Rebus. In 1985 I moved to Tollcross, where in two flats I have stayed ever since, except for brief unsettled stages in Newington, Marchmont again, and the Pink Triangle, the lesbigay *quartier* in and around Broughton Street.

Tollcross

A literary journalist once puzzled me by referring to Norman MacCaig as 'the greatest poet of Tollcross'. Norman lived in Leamington Terrace, downhill from Bruntsfield, and drank in the New Town. Brian McCabe or Dilys Rose (together in Panmure Place) would be sounder nominees.

The exact borders of Tollcross are, however, indeterminate. The cross itself is marked by a clock at the top of Lothian Road where Lauriston, Brougham Place and Leven Street converge. From there 'Tollcross' extends to the edge of the Meadows, that Elysian arena of coarse sporting activity. I think it stretches east along Lauriston as far as the old Royal Infirmary with a sharp border in Lady Lawson Street, where K. Jackson's bar confronts the College of Art and West Port trickles away towards the Grassmarket. Northward, it baulks at the car park facing Castle Rock and terminates short of the former Caledonian, now Hilton Hotel and St John's Church, which are definitely West End. Perhaps debateably, I would extend Tollcross down Morrison Street as far as our local copshop in Torphichen Street, and also along Fountainbridge. It definitely gets as far past the King's Theatre as the Auld Toll Bar and the Golf Tavern before giving way to Bruntsfield, and incorporates the southernmost section of Gilmore Place.

The spine of Tollcross is Lothian Road, where RLS went in his youth to chat up the whores in low drinking dens. Down Bread Street, at right angles, one hits West Port, where Burke and Hare performed their murders and through which Bluidy Clavers, in Scott's great song, 'ganged free' to incite the first Jacobite rising. Nowadays, Tollcross ettles to vie with Paris and Manhattan as a Capital of Culture. We have the Usher Hall, famous for worldclass concerts, two big proscenium arch theatres as well as the Traverse – most famous venue in Britain for experimental drama – two excellent 'arthouse' cinemas and a commercial multiplex. There have been small art galleries abording the three lap-dance and strip-dance pubs which form the celebrated 'Pubic Triangle'. There are brothels (legal in Edinburgh) and clubs, which debouch cheerful revellers out on to Tollcross pavements at three and four in the morning, when some of them fall to stabbing each other. We have a 'High' Pisky church favoured by music-lovers. The famously beautiful Bennet's Bar is only one of many popular hostelries. Italian restaurants vie with Chinese, Thai, Indian and now Japanese. We have busy chippies, too. During August, Tollcross hosts a major Film Festival, the Edinburgh International Festival takes over the Usher Hall and the big theatres, and the Methodist Central Hall houses a festival of youth orchestras, while the Traverse queens it over the rest of the Fringe, which in its own right is the biggest Arts Festival in the World. Trendy persons from London with horrible yah brays invade our familiar resorts, along with perfectly pleasant young people from Notts, Belarus, Botswana etc. Then they all go away and September is invariably the most beautiful month of the year.

The City parentpersons have recently confused our geography by renaming much of Tollcross 'Exchange District'. This is in respect of the recent transformation of Lothian Road by the erection of vast new offices for Standard Life, Clydesdale Bank, Scottish Widows and, most recently, Bank of Scotland. Suits now pour in and out of these premises. Battle for the soul of Tollcross is on between the suits, culturally cloned to eat sensibly, not smoke and buy cars advertised on TV, and the scruffs – the natural Tollcross population of actors, petty criminals, honest artisans, coarse cricketers, sex workers, chip-scoffers, Pakistani shopkeepers, pasta chefs, students, big-screen football addicts, scene shifters, film buffs, Antipodean barmen, kids from the schemes legless on lager or high on eccie, and secondhand booksellers. The outcome of struggle is so far uncertain. Not all the hygienic-looking new takeaway food shops have managed to survive, praise be, but it is ominous that the brothel opposite my flat has doubled in size and gone upmarket, as if suits and whores have signed a separate truce.

Morningside

Very few people nowadays admit to coming from Morningside, a genteel nineteenth century development to the south-west of Edinburgh, notorious as the place where sex was what the coalman used to bring the coal in. But such evasions as 'Bruntsfield' and 'Braid' fool no one. I have to concede that the Morningside Safeways was my favourite supermarket before Morrison's took it over. You got such a good class, or cless, of shopper there.

Hibees and Jamboes

Essentially, Edinburgh is divided between supporters of Hibernian FC, based in Easter Road towards Leith and Heart of Midlothian FC (Hearts = Jam Tarts): 'the Gorgie Boys'. I am relieved that my late father's origins permit me to declare myself a Dundee United supporter.

Big Tam

If my geography above is accepted, the Greatest Living Scotsman is a native son of Tollcross, born in Fountainbridge, though educated in Bruntsfield. Certainly, Tam Connery's first job was as a van laddie – milkman – for the St Cuthbert's Co-operative Society which dominated Edinburgh from Haymarket to West Port in those days. In 'Horace in Tollcross', 007 stands in for Jupiter as well as featuring as a distinguished mortal.

Individual

For Stephen Murray – Joseph Losey directed a very striking movie version of Mozart's Don Giovanni set in Venice.

Echoes of Li He – short bursts of intense imagery distinguish the work of this weird poet (790-816) of the Tang Dynasty.

Curling: Old Murrayfield Ice Rink – before the current dedicated curling rink was built at Murrayfield, curlers used to share ice also used for ice hockey, while skaters wheeled around on the rest of the big old rink. When Sandy Robb delivered one of his 'blooter' takeout shots, lives of young persons skating were endangered.

For Rupsha Fraser – Maurice Ravel the great Basque composer wrote a suite, 'Mother Goose.'

Meeting Mike Janetta and Andy Ross – Mike had been a 'brother curler'. Andy is an expert on Southern African missionary history. The SS *Arandora Star* was torpedoed and sunk off the west coast of Ireland on 2 July 1940. The British Government had interned many thousands of foreign nationals as 'enemy aliens' and this vessel was transporting 1,500 Germans and Italians to Canada. Some were indeed enemies to Britain's cause. Many were innocent, or even proven anti-Fascists.

Thinking About Derek Walcott – in whose epic *Omeros* Homer's

Helen becomes a modern-day proletarian temptress on the island of St Lucia.

Dapper the Day – Zwangendaba was an Nguni chieftain or 'warlord' from what is now KwaZulu Natal who headed away from Shaka's dangerous Zulus, trekked north, and eventually took some of his people as far as the shore of Lake Tanganyika, transforming Southern and Central African ethnography and history on the way. Randolph Turpin, in the 1950s, was the first black boxer from Britain to become a world champion. He came from the English Midlands, and was under discussion while Gary, the barman in Tipplers, was at the door awaiting a sight of his goddess.

Sequence in Cold Spring – Lawley Road features in the South Indian novels of RK Narayan. *Miguel Street* in Port of Spain, Trinidad, is the title and sphere of VS Naipaul's first collection of stories.

Horace in Tollcross

1.31, 4.12 – Ogun is the most versatile and interesting of the Yoruba pantheon of deities, emigrating with slaves from West Africa to become an important presence in Brazil and the Caribbean. He is the artificer god, hence god of creativity, but as blacksmith also god of war. He is god of the road, and hence of carcrashes. I possess a fine statuette of Ogun given to me by the Yoruba sculptor Kasali Akangbe Ogunof.

2.14 – the allusion is not to an educational thinker of the 1960s but to Tolstoy's story 'The Death of Ivan Ilych'.

2.16 – 'Nobody's perfect', said by Joe E. Brown, of course, at the end of *Some Like It Hot*, by a very clear distance the greatest movie ever made.

3.1 – Heather the Weather is the ever-popular lady forecaster for BBC Reporting Scotland TV News.

3.9 – Some readers may need to be informed that Desperate Dan the cowboy addicted to cow pies featured for many years in the *Dandy* comic published by DC Thomson press in Dundee, where there is now a statue to him.

3.30 – James VI of Scotland (Jamie Saxt) named the group of poets he gathered at his court 'the Castalian Band' after a spring on Mount Parnassus sacred to the muses. Zamzamah's restaurant in Lothian Road has now been renamed 'Spice Cottage'.

4.7 – *Wallace* Stevens.

4.8, 4.9 – John Maclean, Marxist, republican and nationalist, was/is one of the legendary heroes of the 'Red Clyde', imprisoned for his opposition to the 1914–18 war, whose reception on his return to Glasgow from jail is commemorated in Hamish Henderson's much sung 'John Maclean March'. In **4.9**, 'May the Twelfth' refers to the swearing in of the first members of the new Scottish Parliament in 1999, when Tommy Sheridan of the Scottish Socialist Party took the oath of loyalty to the Queen under protest, fist raised.

Some other books published by **LUATH** PRESS

The Souls of the Dead are Taking the Best Seats
50 World Poets on War
Compiled by Angus Calder and Beth Junor
ISBN 1 84282 032 X   PB   £7.99

Good war poetry explodes silence

From the clash of steel to the rumble of tanks, the sights and sounds of war have inspired poets of every nation since conflict was invented. In this timely new anthology, respected poet and historian Angus Calder and anti-war activist Beth Junor have drawn together a representation of war poetry from nations and cultures across the globe. Shared experience and powerful imagery combine to give this collection of poems an immediacy and poignancy that illustrate both the horror and the humanity that are distilled by the events that humankind calls war.

I highly recommend this collection of poems: they are as vivid as they are thought-provoking.
– COLONEL CLIVE FAIRWEATHER, CBE,
SCOTTISH APPEAL DIRECTOR, COMBAT STRESS

Scotlands of the Mind
Angus Calder
ISBN 1 84282 008 7   PB   £9.99

Does Scotland as a 'nation' have any real existence? In Britain, in Europe, in the World? Or are there a multitude of multiform 'Scot-lands of the Mind'?

These soul-searching questions are probed in this timely book by prize-winning author and journalist, Angus Calder. Informed and intelligent, this new volume presents the author at his thought-provoking best. The absorbing journey through many possible Scotlands – fictionalised, idealised, and politicised – is sure to fascinate.

This perceptive and often highly personal writing shows the breathtaking scope of Calder's analytical power. Fact or fiction, individual or international, politics or poetry, statistics or statehood, no subject is taboo in a volume that offers an overview of the vicissitudes and changing nature of Scottishness.

Through mythical times to manufactured histories, from Empire and Diaspora, from John Knox to Home Rule and beyond, Calder shatters literary, historical and cultural misconceptions and provides invaluable insights into the Scottish psyche. Offering a fresh understanding of an ever-evolving Scotland, *Scotlands of the Mind* contributes to what Calder himself has called 'the needful getting of a new act together'.

Thoughtful and provocative, Calder is among the best essayists of today.
Bernard Crick, THE GUARDIAN

Angus Calder has proved himself one of the most sophisticated thinkers and writers on the gleaming new Scotland.
THE SCOTSMAN

POETRY

Burning Whins
Liz Niven
ISBN 1 84282 074 5 PB £8.99

Drink the Green Fairy
Brian Whittingham
ISBN 1 84282 020 6 PB £8.99

Tartan & Turban
Bashabi Fraser
ISBN 1 84282 044 3 PB £8.99

The Ruba'iyat of Omar Khayyam, in Scots
Rab Wilson
ISBN 1 84282 046 X PB £8.99

Talking with Tongues
Brian D. Finch
ISBN 1 84282 006 0 PB £8.99

Kate o Shanter's Tale and other poems [book]
Matthew Fitt
ISBN 1 84282 028 1 PB £6.99

Kate o Shanter's Tale and other poems [audio CD]
Matthew Fitt
ISBN 1 84282 043 5 PB £9.99

Bad Ass Raindrop
Kokumo Rocks
ISBN 1 84282 018 4 PB £6.99

Madame Fifi's Farewell and other poems
Gerry Cambridge
ISBN 1 84282 005 2 PB £8.99

Poems to be Read Aloud
introduced by Tom Atkinson
ISBN 0 946487 00 6 PB £5.00

Scots Poems to be Read Aloud
introduced by Stuart McHardy
ISBN 0 946487 81 2 PB £5.00

Picking Brambles
Des Dillon
ISBN 1 84282 021 4 PB £6.99

Sex, Death & Football
Alistair Findlay
ISBN 1 84282 022 2 PB £6.99

The Luath Burns Companion
John Cairney
ISBN 1 84282 000 1 PB £10.00

Immortal Memories: A Compilation of Toasts to the Memory of Burns as delivered at Burns Suppers, 1801-2001
John Cairney
ISBN 1 84282 009 5 HB £20.00

The Whisky Muse: Scotch whisky in poem & song
Robin Laing
ISBN 1 84282 041 9 PB £7.99

A Long Stride Shortens the Road
Donald Smith
ISBN 1 84282 073 7 PB £8.99

Into the Blue Wavelengths
Roderick Watson
ISBN 1 84282 075 3 PB £8.99

The Souls of the Dead are Taking the Best Seats: 50 World Poets on War
Compiled by Angus Calder and Beth Junor
ISBN 1 84282 032 X PB £7.99

FICTION

Torch
Lin Anderson
ISBN 1 84282 042 7 PB £9.99

Heartland
John MacKay
ISBN 1 84282 059 1 PB £9.99

The Blue Moon Book
Anne MacLeod
ISBN 1 84282 061 3 PB £9.99

The Glasgow Dragon
Des Dillon
ISBN 1 84282 056 7 PB £9.99

Driftnet
Lin Anderson
ISBN 1 84282 034 6 PB £9.99

The Fundamentals of New Caledonia
David Nicol
ISBN 1 84282 93 6 HB £16.99

Milk Treading
Nick Smith
ISBN 1 84282 037 0 PB £6.99

The Road Dance
John MacKay
ISBN 1 84282 024 9 PB £6.99

The Strange Case of RL Stevenson
Richard Woodhead
ISBN 0 946487 86 3 HB £16.99

But n Ben A-Go-Go
Matthew Fitt
ISBN 0 946487 82 0 HB £10.99
ISBN 1 84282 014 1 PB £6.99

The Bannockburn Years
William Scott
ISBN 0 946487 34 0 PB £7.95

Outlandish Affairs: An Anthology of Amorous Encounters
Edited and introduced by Evan Rosenthal and Amanda Robinson
ISBN 1 84282 055 9 PB £9.99

LANGUAGE

Luath Scots Language Learner [Book]
L Colin Wilson
ISBN 0 946487 91 X PB £9.99

Luath Scots Language Learner [Double Audio CD Set]
L Colin Wilson
ISBN 1 84282 026 5 CD £16.99

WALK WITH LUATH

Mountain Days & Bothy Nights
Dave Brown and Ian Mitchell
ISBN 0 946487 15 4 PB £7.50

The Joy of Hillwalking
Ralph Storer
ISBN 1 84282 069 9 PB £7.50

Scotland's Mountains before the Mountaineers
Ian R. Mitchell
ISBN 0 946487 39 1 PB £9.99

Mountain Outlaw
Ian R. Mitchell
ISBN 1 84282 027 3 PB £6.50

POLITICS & CURRENT ISSUES

Scotlands of the Mind
Angus Calder
ISBN 1 84282 008 7 PB £9.99

Trident on Trial: the case for people's disarmament
Angie Zelter
ISBN 1 84282 004 4 PB £9.99

Uncomfortably Numb: A Prison Requiem
Maureen Maguire
ISBN 1 84282 001 X PB £8.99

Scotland: Land & Power – the Agenda for Land Reform
Andy Wightman
ISBN 0 946487 70 7 PB £5.00

Old Scotland New Scotland
Jeff Fallow
ISBN 0 946487 40 5 PB £6.99

Some Assembly Required: Behind the scenes at the Re-birth of the Scottish Parliament
David Shepherd
ISBN 0 946487 84 7 PB £7.99

Notes from the North Incorporating a brief history of the Scots and the English
Emma Wood
ISBN 0 946487 46 4 PB £8.99

Scotlands of the Future: sustainability in a small nation
ed Eurig Scandrett
ISBN 1 84282 035 4 PB £7.99

Eurovision or American Dream? Britain, the Euro and the Future of Europe
David Purdy
ISBN 1 84282 036 2 PB £3.99

Luath Press Limited
committed to publishing well written books worth reading

LUATH PRESS takes its name from Robert Burns, whose little collie Luath (*Gael.*, swift or nimble) tripped up Jean Armour at a wedding and gave him the chance to speak to the woman who was to be his wife and the abiding love of his life. Burns called one of *The Twa Dogs* Luath after Cuchullin's hunting dog in *Ossian's Fingal*. Luath Press was established in 1981 in the heart of Burns country, and is now based a few steps up the road from Burns' first lodgings on Edinburgh's Royal Mile. Luath offers you distinctive writing with a hint of unexpected pleasures.

Most bookshops in the UK, the US, Canada, Australia, New Zealand and parts of Europe either carry our books in stock or can order them for you. To order direct from us, please send a £sterling cheque, postal order, international money order or your credit card details (number, address of cardholder and expiry date) to us at the address below. Please add post and packing as follows: UK – £1.00 per delivery address; overseas surface mail – £2.50 per delivery address; overseas airmail – £3.50 for the first book to each delivery address, plus £1.00 for each additional book by airmail to the same address. If your order is a gift, we will happily enclose your card or message at no extra charge.

Luath Press Limited
543/2 Castlehill
The Royal Mile
Edinburgh EH1 2ND
Scotland
Telephone: 0131 225 4326 (24 hours)
Fax: 0131 225 4324
email: gavin.macdougall@luath.co.uk
Website: www.luath.co.uk